The Reading Advantage

Quick & Easy Ways to Transform Your Child into a Passionate Reader!

The Reading Advantage

Quick & Easy Ways to Transform Your Child into a Passionate Reader!

Strawberry Shakespeare

Diamond Star Press

Los Angeles

The Reading Advantage: Quick & Easy Ways To Transform Your Child Into A Passionate Reader!

Copyright © 2018 S. F. Howe
Published by Diamond Star Press

First Paperback Edition
ISBN 13: 978-1-7324591-3-7
ISBN 10: 1-73245-913-4

Children's Books by Strawberry Shakespeare

NOVELS

Saving Bluestone Belle

Hope's Horse: The Mystery of Shadow Ridge

SHORT STORY COLLECTIONS

The Cloud Horse & Other Stories

BOX SETS

The 3-Volume Horse Kid Series:
Saving Bluestone Belle, Hope's Horse, The Cloud Horse

SCREENPLAYS

Family Comedy-Adventure

Saving Bluestone Belle

Free Gift

THE APPALOOSA COLT
by
Strawberry Shakespeare

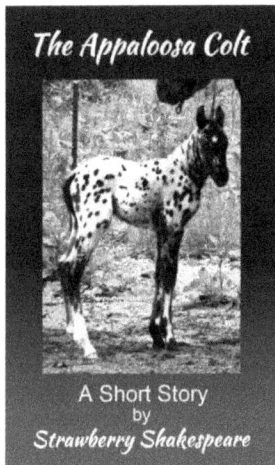

When young Katie begins a volunteer job at the local horse rescue, her life changes in an amazing way. You'll take the journey with Katie as she goes from the painful low of an unjust accusation to the high of an impossible dream coming true; all of this while she is also awakening to her extraordinary ability with horses – a gift she never knew she had!

As our thanks to all the caring parents who have read *The Reading Advantage: Quick & Easy Ways to Transform Your Child into a Passionate Reader!*, we would like you to have the bonus short fiction ebook, "The Appaloosa Colt." This charming selection from Strawberry Shakespeare's bestselling short story collection for ages 8-12, *The Cloud Horse & Other Stories*, is certain to delight horse kids of all ages. Go to http://bit.ly/theappaloosacolt to download your free ebook now.

For all the parents who patiently nurture their children's love of reading

Table of Contents

Introduction

How to Gain the Reading Advantage

Research has found that a child who reads books tends to become a more educated, successful and prosperous adult. The main purpose of this book is twofold: to reveal how you can increase your child's interest in reading and to support you in making the necessary changes that will improve your child's reading behavior.

By our definition, the best children's books tell positive, edifying stories while keeping kids glued to the page and entertained. We hope the information in this guide inspires you to spend time exploring the great reading material that is available and helps you choose the books your kids will love.

In addition, we show you how to facilitate family bonding by selecting books that are suitable for all ages and can be read aloud to the whole family. Reading books aloud is one of the most beneficial and enjoyable activities your family can share.

This guide further reveals the unique needs of reluctant readers and aims to encourage parents to deal more effectively with the reluctant reader in their midst. By understanding the needs of reluctant readers and seeking out those special books that a reluctant reader will love, your kid can be transformed into a passionate reader. To that end, we have included a chapter from *Saving Bluestone Belle*, a novel for ages 8-12, as an example of writing that appeals to both reluctant readers and avid readers.

We also aimed to fill this little book with tips and tricks parents can use in everyday life to increase a child's interest in reading. Establishing any new habits and behaviors, even those necessary for helping your child become a more avid reader, can be challenging. But we show you how to make it easy by just doing a little at a time. The good news is small changes do yield big results.

Finally, we have included an important research analysis by the National Education Association on the effects of reading books on child development. This is essential reading for every parent.

As both a psychologist and the author of three books for young readers, Strawberry Shakespeare has made it her business to uplift, enlighten and thoroughly entertain children with her writing. Whether you are reading aloud to the whole family or encouraging your child to read for pleasure, we invite you to select from among her trio of standalone children's horse books. Her motto is 'no child will be left behind.'

Our own teacher survey reveals that these books delight both reluctant and avid readers, and that kids are swept away by the excitement, action and heart coursing through these volumes.

At the end of this book, you will find more information about Strawberry Shakespeare's children's books and how to order them. Or you can visit www.StrawberryShakespeare.com for immediate access to these timeless treasures.

In the next chapter, the author shares her personal story about her reading history and how one person's interest in encouraging her to read profoundly affected he entire life.

Chapter 1

My Personal Story

My mother taught me how to read when I was four years old, and I can never thank her enough for giving me that amazing gift. There could have been no better teacher than my mother. Not only was she an avid reader who carved time out of every busy day to read books, but she was also a born educator whose childhood dream was to teach elementary school.

Unfortunately, that dream was never to be fulfilled. She had to go out into the world to work as the eldest of three, though still but a child herself, in order to help supplement the family income after her father's sudden death.

My mother never became a teacher in the conventional sense, but her gift for teaching and passion for reading shined through in every moment of our time together. With such a brilliant teacher, I quickly became a star pupil and was reading at an advanced level by the age of five.

Throughout middle school and high school, I would passionately consume the classics of world literature the way other kids studied fashion or sports magazines. With my reading advantage, I skipped two grades and graduated high school at sixteen. I would go on to complete a master's degree and four years of doctoral training in clinical psychology.

My mother did everything right when it came to encouraging my love of reading. She taught me how to read not because of any personal agenda, but because I pestered her relentlessly to teach me. You see, at that time I wanted to be like my big sister in every way; and my sister had been receiving in-home tutoring while she recovered from an illness.

Once I started reading, my mother may have suggested certain titles, but she never tried to control my reading choices or when or how much I read. Instead, she demonstrated her own love of reading by reading books herself, taking me to the library often, reading stories to me, giving me gifts of books and magazine subscriptions, displaying her own books in an attractive bookcase in the living room and providing me with a bookcase for my books. She even created a project for the two of us where we lovingly repainted that bookcase from time to time to keep up its fresh appearance.

My love of reading continues to brighten my life to this day. It has contributed to my becoming the author of more than nine non-fiction books and three children's fiction books. I owe it all to my mother's love of reading and to her innate talent, endless patience and unfailing devotion to teaching a rambunctious little four-year-old how to read.

In the following chapter, you will learn the single best and easiest way to encourage your child to read.

Chapter 2

It Begins with You

You probably know that your children use the parent of the same sex as their primary role model. But did you know that they are not affected so much by what you say as what you do? Children are like little sponges, absorbing all that happens around them and storing in their memory banks images of you and how you live. Everything you do offers an example to your child of how an adult behaves and what it means to be an adult. It is no different when it comes to reading books. Seeking out excellent books for kids and giving them the gift of a great read is important, but it is not the only way to help your child enjoy reading. Another way is to give your child the memory of *you* reading books.

Do your children see you quietly reading books or magazines? If so, you have contributed mightily to their appreciation and love of reading. Do your children go with you to the library or bookstore and watch you search for and acquire books? If so, you are imprinting upon their minds the indelible image that adults seek out and value books.

Demonstrating your own love of reading is the greatest encouragement for reading that you can offer your child. If there is a resistance to reading in your child, look to yourself and most especially to the parent who is the same gender as the child. For example, a boy who is a reluctant reader often has a father who has either pushed him to read books that he does not enjoy or who is himself a non-reader.

Children will often respond with avoidance and withdrawal when feeling pressured to read, even if the pressure is sensed and not spoken. Similarly, they will pick up on your lack of interest in reading subconsciously and, out of their love for you and natural desire to be like you, will imitate that.

Your sincere love of books and reading will automatically be conveyed to your children at a subconscious level. Be aware of how important you are in shaping every aspect of your child's future, including their love of reading. Give your child the gift of a high quality life filled with the ongoing enjoyment and exploration reading books provides. Seek out the best books for kids and read books aloud to your family. Better yet, be a reader yourself and you will have a family of readers.

In the following chapter, we explore reading books aloud and why it plays such an important role in increasing your child's interest in reading.

Chapter 3

Why Read Books Aloud

Being read to is one of childhood's favorite activities. All those precious moments of reading to your child before bedtime or when they are ill are impressed upon their young minds, merging the telling of enjoyable tales with a parent's love and care. So what better way to unify your family than to read books aloud as a whole family?

Everyone loves a story, and your family is no different. When you read books aloud to your family, you enjoy a marvelous shared experience. Not only does it afford enjoyable time together for a unified purpose, but it also provides an opportunity to discuss the values and choices expressed in the story while helping to focus attention on positive and wholesome solutions to the problems of life.

How do you find children's books that can be enjoyed by the whole family? There are many books suitable for reading aloud to the whole family, including numerous classics of children's literature. In the offline world, your local librarian is a wonderful resource in your search. Online, enjoy the wealth of options on Amazon.com.

Whatever book you choose to read aloud to your family, know that you are helping your family grow closer through this shared experience. In your discussions about the books or stories, you are reaffirming the values you hold most dearly. And perhaps most importantly, when you read books aloud as a family it instills an appreciation and love of reading in your children. And what greater gift is there?

In Chapter 4, we explore the third most important factor for transforming your child into a passionate reader

Chapter 4

The Pleasure Principle

No matter what your kid's past behavior has been in regard to reading – total avoidance, full enjoyment or anything in between – in selecting books for kids you can be certain they will gladly read books that bring them pleasure. Whether it's allowing their imagination to soar in a fantasy tale, feeling the excitement of adventure in an action-oriented story, enjoying the fun and laughter of a humorous fable, or being compelled to turn the pages of a suspenseful saga; pleasure is what drives reading in kids.

By understanding this basic concept, you can find high quality books for kids that offer some or all of the above features. As a result, you will suddenly discover that your child is reading like a champ or seems more motivated to overcome their reading weaknesses. And isn't that what it's all about? A lifelong love of reading and learning, as you know, produces a more intelligent, more financially successful and more socially effective adult.

So start with the idea of pleasure in selecting books for your child, and you won't go wrong. That does not mean you need to throw quality out the window. Pleasure and quality can and do exist hand and hand, if you choose wisely. Ideally, you want to give your child books that they will enjoy and which will also edify them in some way. But the problem with the books your child has rejected in the past is that they are missing the pleasure factor.

Did you know that the brain does not complete its structural development until the age of 25? It's true – your child will continue to develop their mental powers throughout adolescence and into young adulthood. They will eventually find their own way in choosing and enjoying books. However, until kids discover for themselves the importance of reading and are internally motivated to read, you can cultivate their attraction to reading by identifying books that will bring them pleasure and seek to provide those types of books for your child.

Allow yourself to let go of the idea that your children should force themselves to read books that have undeniable quality but which they do not enjoy, and instead let them find their own level in reading, even if this means comic books or graphic novels. This is the route to developing a dedicated and avid reader in adulthood. Don't be afraid you'll create an adult who only reads comic books if you allow reading pleasure to come first in childhood.

The next chapter addresses one of the most confounding issues for parents: the reluctant reader, and provides seven strategic tips for overcoming your child's resistance to reading.

Chapter 5

How to Select a Book for a Reluctant Reader

Reluctant readers come in two basic varieties: kids who have good reading skills but don't like to read and kids who are so challenged by reading, they avoid it as much as possible. The following seven suggestions address the needs of both types of readers.

LIGHTEN UP

The number one way to overcome a child's reluctance to read is to choose stories that are light in narrative and strong in action and dialogue. Best of all are fast-moving tales filled with suspense and humor. Kids lose their resistance to reading when they are swept away by a story that makes them laugh with delight and keeps them glued to the page wondering what's going to happen next.

AGE-APPROPRIATE CONTENT

When weak readers are given books suitable for their reading level, the content level is often too low. This causes the child to quickly lose interest in reading. Until the marketplace offers more hi/lo books, which meet a child at their reading level while also sustaining their interest, err on the side of choosing books with age-appropriate content.

YOU CAN TELL A BOOK BY ITS COVER

The book cover is critical in attracting the interest of a reluctant reader. The cover art needs to be sophisticated and visually stimulating, hinting at the humor and excitement that lies within. Avoid books with covers that seem to "talk down" to your child.

LEAN AND MEAN

The interior book design can make or break your child's willingness to tackle a book. Text pages should be lean, with somewhat larger print, plenty of margin and comfortable spacing between letters and lines. There is nothing less appealing to a reluctant reader than full pages of small, tightly set print.

SHORT AND SWEET

The presentation of the content is important as well for sustaining the attention of a reluctant reader. Give a child a sense of progress and speed in moving through the book and you engage their interest. Therefore, total page count, as well as individual chapters, paragraphs and sentences, should all be on the shorter side.

A PICTURE SAYS A THOUSAND WORDS

Illustrations are desirable because they break up the text while helping to fill gaps in the reader's comprehension. The entertainment value of illustrations should not be overlooked, as they add enjoyment and interest to the reading experience.

OKAY, SO IT'S NOT A BOOK

While audio books might seem like a cop-out for children struggling with reading, they should be considered for their educational and entertainment value and because they will enable the reluctant reader to keep up with the crowd and perform better in class. Ditto for graphic novels, which tell a story through illustrations and dialogue, making comprehension easy.

If you keep these seven suggestions in mind when selecting a book for your reluctant reader, you will help optimize your child's reading enjoyment and sense of accomplishment. Every positive experience your child has with reading encourages him to do more reading, and isn't that what it's all about?

If your child is a reluctant reader, we highly recommend Strawberry Shakespeare's award-winning, horse-themed novel for ages 8-12,

Saving Bluestone Belle. We provide a sample of this book in the next chapter because it illustrates the type of writing that appeals to a reluctant reader.

Chapter 6

Reluctant Readers Sampler

This chapter provides an example of the type of fiction writing that is proven to appeal to reluctant readers ages 8-12. The following excerpt meets six out of the seven criteria specified in the previous chapter. The seventh is not applicable because it refers to audiobooks and graphic novels.

In this sample from Strawberry Shakespeare's illustrated comic-adventure novel, *Saving Bluestone Belle*, ten-year-old rich kid, Homer Easton, accompanied by his wacky entourage – housekeeper Maria, psychiatrist Dr. Willoughby, and personal trainer Joe – have hit the road, in pursuit of the thieves that stole Homer's beloved horse, Blue.

Chapter 3: The Mysterious Map

Driving the Mercedes east through sizzling desert, Joe forced his eyes to stay open while the other three passengers dozed. He finally pulled into a truck stop and the four drowsily trudged into the restaurant. They slid into a booth and a bus boy dumped menus on the table.

A stoop-shouldered waitress with a hangdog face shuffled over. "Are you ready?"

Maria didn't open the menu. "*Agua, mucho* ice."

Joe looked up from his menu. "Is that all you're going to have?"

"*Si*, I no have *pesos*."

"This could be our last meal today. Order anything you want, it's on me."

Maria smiled gratefully at Joe and told the waitress, "*Enchiladas grandes con* extra *chiles y un* side of *guacamole*, hold the sour *crema*—"

The waitress jotted it down, then quirked an expectant eyebrow at Joe.

"*—y un chocolate* malted, *muy frio, con* two *grandes* poufs of whippy *crema*," finished a glowing Maria.

The waitress turned back to her with a sour face. "Anything else?"

Maria shrugged gleefully. "This is my last supper."

"Right," said the waitress, moving on to Dr. Willoughby. "And you, mister?"

"A rare burger with everything."

She looked at Joe.

"Same, but hold the onions."

The waitress studied Homer, who sat pale and shrunken in his despair. "And you, little man?"

Homer grimaced. "I'm not hungry."

Maria eyed him, her brow knotted with worry. "You have to eat. It make you strong."

"I can't, not until we find Blue."

"How about just a little something?" encouraged Dr. Willoughby.

Homer shook his head.

"He'll have a hot dog, and we'll also have four tuna sandwiches to go," said Dr. Willoughby.

As the group waited in silence for their food, Homer glanced out the window. Lo and behold, he spotted a blue pickup with a red horse trailer stationed at the far end of the restaurant parking lot.

"Look!" Homer whispered, pointing stealthily.

The others took in the truck then scanned the room for suspicious characters. Surly and sleazy-looking *hombres* occupied every seat in the house.

"They're here somewhere," said Homer.

The meals arrived and the quartet ate with their eyes on the other customers. Suddenly, Joe jumped up and headed for the rear of the restaurant. He slipped out a back door.

Seconds later, the three at the table saw him creep over to the truck. They watched as he wrestled with the unyielding trailer door then disappeared into the cab.

"What's that idiot doing?" hissed Dr. Willoughby. "He could get himself killed."

Homer looked on, fascinated.

"Aye yih yih," Maria groaned.

Two grizzled men, one pudgy, the other skinny, rose from the counter, plunked down cash, and left. Through the window, Homer, Maria, and Dr. Willoughby observed them saunter toward the back of the parking lot, heading for the pickup truck.

Maria rolled her eyes heavenward, praying fervently. *"Dios que esta en el cielo—"*

Dr. Willoughby touched her arm, bringing her back to reality. "Follow me. Act normal."

He went to the cashier and paid the bill. His jaw dropped when Maria and Homer whistled, shoved their hands in their pockets, and tap danced out of the restaurant.

Once outside, the three scooted to the back. They peered around the corner of the restaurant just as the two thieves entered the pickup.

All was eerily quiet. Inside the truck, nothing moved. The trio sneaked over and chanced a peek inside. The two scruffy men sprawled across the front seat, unconscious, while Joe rummaged through the glove compartment.

Joe removed something and jumped out of the truck.

"Are you crazy?" cried Dr. Willoughby.

Joe studied his find. "I don't know, Einstein, you tell me." He shoved a piece of ragged parchment in Dr. Willoughby's face. "It's all here," said Joe, slapping the paper.

Bug-eyed, Maria and Homer craned their necks to see. They glimpsed a mysterious map with crude renderings of a four leaf clover, a boat on waves, an infinity sign, a sombrero, and a hatchet!

"What is?" sniffed Dr. Willoughby.

The guys in the truck stirred. "They're coming to," Joe breathed, then gestured to everyone to be quiet and follow him. The group tiptoed away, hunching over to make themselves as small as possible, and reentered the restaurant through the back door.

Rocco and Bart stumbled out of the truck, rubbing their foreheads where each sported a large purple bump.

"What happened?" whimpered Rocco.

"I don't know."

Scowling, they scanned the area for anything suspicious, but all was still.

"We'd better get going," said Bart, "or Crawford will kill us."

Rocco started up the truck and pulled out onto the road while Bart sorted through the glove compartment. Soon, he was flinging its contents helter-skelter.

"What are you doing?"

"It's missing," cried Bart.

"I didn't hear that," Rocco growled.

"I'm telling you, it's gone."

Rocco made a wide, skidding U-turn and raced back to the diner. A highway patrolman surfaced from out of the shadows and followed, hot on their tail.

Dr. Willoughby's black Mercedes cruised by the truck, heading in the opposite direction. Joe, Maria, and Homer winked and grinned at Rocco and Bart.

"Don't smile at them!" yelled Dr. Willoughby.

But it was too late. Rocco and Bart looked at each other and nodded. Glowering, Rocco tore into another U-turn then spotted the flashing lights of the motorcycle cop.

A loudspeaker blared, "Pull over and stop your truck. Pull over and stop your truck."

The pickup glided to a halt and the cop rolled in right behind.

The black Mercedes disappeared down the road with the three back seat passengers glued to the rear window, watching as the cop issued Rocco a ticket.

"Yes!" exulted Homer.

The three turned forward in unison, strengthened in their resolve. They would make this mission a success!

End of Excerpt

We hope you enjoyed this excerpt from *Saving Bluestone Belle* by Strawberry Shakespeare. In the following chapter, we offer our list of 21 easy ways to increase your child's interest in reading.

Chapter 7

Twenty-One Ways to Interest Your Child in Reading

You are certain to find many ideas in this chapter that will help you encourage your child to read. These methods work together to convey a consistent message about the joy of reading and the importance of books. An attitude of experimentation is best until you find the special combination that unlocks the passionate reader within your child. This information is geared toward parents, but can also apply well to teachers if you think "classroom" instead of "home."

1. Does your child know without the slightest shadow of a doubt that you care about reading? Is your child getting the same positive message about reading from the other adults in their lives, including relatives, caretakers and teachers? Conveying consistently to your child how valuable and meaningful reading is to you shapes how your child feels about reading. Science has determined that a child's positive attitude toward reading is the single most important element in determining their interest in reading.

2. Pressuring your child to read every day has been shown to yield no results in improving a child's interest in reading and may even increase a child's resistance to reading books. The research data indicates that this affects all types of reading, including books that they are reading for pleasure. The feeling of being forced to read is counter-productive to your child's development of a love of reading. Consider adding a silent family reading time to your day, where everyone gathers to enjoy reading the material of their choice. Let your child read whatever he or

she selects without your judgment or interference.

3. If you want to encourage your child to read, experts recommend that you give your child a weekly book and magazine allowance. This allowance should be in addition to any other weekly monies you give to your child. Even a small amount that allows for one purchase per week will succeed in boosting your child's interest in reading.

4. Take your child to your favorite newsstand or local bookstore to explore the magazine rack with the intention of making a purchase. While you may need to provide gentle guidance to help your child make an age-appropriate selection, it is essential, in order for this practice to work, that you show respect for your child's choice of reading matter and that you follow through and purchase it for them. In so doing, you further encourage their love of reading.

5. Kids love to receive magazine subscriptions in the mail. They feel important and excited

when they receive mail of any kind, and even more so if it's a colorful magazine on one of their favorite subjects. So include one or more magazine subscriptions in your dedicated plan to encourage your child to read.

6. Providing a bookcase, shelving, or other storage for books in your child's room is essential for helping your child to value his books and experience the pride of ownership. It is best to have it occupy a prominent place in the room, rather than be located out of sight, such as inside a closet, as it makes the books visible to him and easily accessible. Also, make sure your child puts his name inside his books as it further enhances his pride in owning these books.

7. Not only should your children have a dedicated place for their books, your books of quality should also have a place where they are clearly displayed in the house to signify the idea that books are important in your home.

8. Does your child enjoy visiting the library? Whether she does or not, it helps to be a family

that loves the library and makes frequent visits. Let your child be as interested or disinterested as may be the case, but bring her to the library while you search for great books for yourself. You may be surprised at how quickly your kid starts selecting her own books to take out.

9. Let the librarians at your school and local library help interest your child in books. Librarians love to assist kids in finding great reading material. Their knowledge of age-appropriate books can't be beat, and getting them involved can aid your cause to encourage your child to read. One way to engage librarians is to introduce them to your child and have them suggest something to read that your kid will enjoy.

10. Proposing specific reading material to your child is another tool in your reading toolbox. Don't hesitate to recommend specific books to your child, maybe books you loved as a child or new releases that sound just right for him. All you need do is make sure your child understands what type of read it will be, e.g.,

easy, difficult, fast, slow, and let him make his own decision.

11. Be permissive with your child's reading behavior when it comes to starting and finishing books. Your child should never be forced to finish a book he is reading for pleasure, anymore than you would want to force yourself to finish a book you started reading for pleasure but are not enjoying. Mild encouragement to keep going might be given initially, with the explanation that sometimes it takes a while to get caught up in a story, but never push your kid to keep reading something they dislike.

12. Do your children know that you buy books for yourself and enjoy reading them? If you don't buy books and read, then this is a good time to start, as it is one of the most direct ways to encourage your child to read more books.

13. Sometimes your child may want to read aloud to you or the family. If so this is a golden opportunity to stop everything, give him full

attention, and let him read to you in his own way, at his own pace, while you listen patiently.

14. With technology at the forefront of everyday life, your child's reading is likely to include content on the internet. Assist your child to find sites and material to read in their areas of interest. You can also browse with them on Amazon, where they can look at the book cover images, read the descriptions of myriad books, and check out the samples within the 'Look Inside' of the books that most appeal to them until they find something they would love to read.

15. Your child's talents, interests and hobbies should be supported by you. Any one of them, if not all, can be advantageous to your goal of increasing your child's interest in reading. All you have to do is give them, or help them select, books and magazines that feed their passions. You can even do this without breaking the bank. An abundance of great, inexpensive reading material can be found online or via sales at new

or used bookstores or in used book sales at your library.

16. Your child is just waiting to be praised by you for doing something right. Do you make sure to catch the big and little things they do every day that show their wonderful qualities? One important thing to notice is your child's reading behavior, Try to find ways to praise them and/or acknowledge them for even the smallest improvements in their reading, such as spending more time reading, or showing more interest in reading, as well as praise for finishing a long book or a difficult reading assignment. Kids desperately want their parents' love and approval and respond beautifully to your praise and acknowledgement.

17. Feed your child's natural curiosity and innate intelligence by providing books and other reading material about the significant events that are affecting the whole family, and then discuss it with them. On the positive side, this could be a travel book related to an upcoming vacation or a

how-to book on caring for a new pet. On the opposite end of the spectrum, a book that helps kids adjust to a move, a loss, or other stressful change in their lives not only supports their interest in reading but provides an excellent opening for them to reveal their deeper thoughts and feelings.

18. Don't overlook the opportunity to bond with your child and support their love of reading by reading a book along with your child when they are assigned to read something for school or when they choose to read a book for pleasure. This gives you a chance to have discussions with your child about the book and for both of you to share your ideas and responses to what you are reading.

19. Research has found that when you and your child make something together, such as following a recipe to bake a pie, or constructing something from a kit, such as a model airplane, the result is better if your child reads the directions rather than you reading it to him, or even

better, if he reads them aloud. So let your next project be the perfect occasion to encourage your child to read the instructions aloud, and both of you will benefit from the results.

20. With nearly constant attention to devices rampant in our culture, and with your child's ready access to mobile devices such as smart phones and tablets, let their time online be spent productively by helping them seek out exciting online reading programs and games that are designed to stimulate a child's reading and thinking abilities.

21. In line with our previous mention of devices, why not give your child the most amazing gift of all, an ebook reader, such as a Kindle. These devices, as you may well know, allow children to access and read books in a safe area managed by their parents. Amazon offers a variety of options including Kindle FreeTime in the US and Kindle for Kids in the UK.

The following chapter should be read carefully as it offers research data on reading behavior in children that confirms the value and meaning of the suggestions presented in this guide. Also note in numbers 1 and 3 how important the role of the parent is for a child's success in school.

Chapter 8

Research on Children's Reading Behavior

I n this chapter, we have included information from the National Education Association that says it all about the importance of reading for a child's successful development. If you ever doubted the value of reading for your child's success, the significance of their reading for fun or the need for your ongoing involvement in your child's reading life, the following research results should help put any doubts to rest.

Facts About Children's Literacy

1) Children who are read to at home have a higher success rate in school.

According to the National Center for Education Statistics (NCES), a division of the U.S. Department of Education[1], children who are read to at home enjoy a substantial advantage over children who are not:

Twenty-six percent of children who were read to three or four times in the last week by a family member recognized all letters of the alphabet. This is compared to 14 percent of children who were read to less frequently.

The NCES[1] also reported that children who were read to frequently are also more likely to:

- count to 20, or higher than those who were not (60% vs. 44%)
- write their own names (54% vs. 40%)
- read or pretend to read (77% vs. 57%)

According to NCES[2], only 53 percent of children ages three to five were read to daily by a family member (1999). Children in families with incomes below the poverty line are less likely to be read to aloud everyday than are children in families with incomes at or above poverty.

The more types of reading materials there are in the home, the higher students are in reading proficiency, according to the Educational Testing Service.[3]

The Educational Testing Services reported that students who do more reading at home are better readers and have higher math scores; however, students read less for fun as they get older.[3]

2) Children who read frequently develop stronger reading skills.

According to the National Education Association, having kids read a lot is one of the crucial components of becoming a good reader. Young readers need to become practiced at recognizing letters and sounds. The only way to get good at it is to practice.[4]

The U.S. Department of Education[5] found that, generally, the more students read for fun on their own time, the higher their reading scores. Between 1984 and 1996, however, the percentage of 12th grade students reporting that they "never" or "hardly ever" read for fun increased from 9 percent to 16 percent.

A poll of middle and high school students commissioned by the National Education Association[6] found that 56 percent of young people say they read more than 10 books a year, with middle school students reading the most. Some 70 percent of middle school students read more than 10 books a year, compared with only 49 percent of high school students.

3) Other facts

The substantial relationship between parent involvement with the school and reading comprehension levels of fourth-grade classrooms is obvious, according to the U.S. Department of Education.[7] Where parent involvement is low, the classroom mean average (reading score) is 46 points below the national average. Where involvement is high, classrooms score 28 points above the national average - a gap of 74 points. Even after controlling for other attributes of communities, schools, principals, classes, and students, that might confound this relationship, the gap is 44 points.

The National Assessment of Educational Progress[8] tested children nationwide for reading skills. The results for reading tests for fourth-grade students were: Below the most basic level 38 percent; Proficient 31 percent, and Advanced 7 percent.

[1]U.S. Department of Education, National Center for Education Statistics, 2000.

[2]U.S. Department of Education, National Center for Education Statistics, from http://www.nces.ed.gov/fastfacts/display.asp?id+56.

[3]Educational Testing Service, 1999. *America's Smallest School:* The Family.

[4]Gutloff, Karen. 1999, January. "Reading Research Ready to Go." NEA Today. Washington, DC: National Education Association.

[5]U.S. Department of Education. 1999. *The Condition of Education* 1998.

[6]Poll commissioned for the National Education Association by Peter D. Hart Research Associates, February 2001.

[7]U.S. Department of Education. 1996. *Reading Literacy* in the United States: Findings From the IEA Reading Literacy Study.

[8]U.S. Department of Education, National Center for Education Statistics, 1999, March. The Executive Summary of the *1998 National Assessment of Educational Progress* Reading Report Card for the Nation, NCES 1999-50, Washington, DC.

Conclusion

The Benefits of Change

Change is difficult for everyone, and that is no different even for a parent who is concerned about their child's lack of interest in reading. It is only human nature that we tend to hold on to our existing beliefs and practices until something causes us to reach critical mass. This can be an unfortunate event that shocks someone into change or it can be a quiet moment in time when enough input has been absorbed such that a change happens effortlessly.

The problem with both of these methods of change is that in the first case, you are forced to take action because of an unwanted development, and in the second case, action may be delayed until it is too late. We are sure you would agree that it is best to take action when the problem is first noted rather than ignore it until it develops into a severe issue.

Making the most of the many ways to encourage your child to read books begins right now with your recognition and appreciation of the importance of reading. If you haven't fully integrated the importance of reading as a key to your child's future success in life, then our recommendations can be easily discounted, or you may find yourself resisting taking action on the suggestions and tips offered in this guide.

In the typical scenario, a parent may consume this short read, get interested in or excited about certain ideas, but then put the book aside and, given the nature of our busy lives, turn their attention to something else, forgetting completely about what it is they just read. Without the necessary follow through, that parent remains stuck in an unchanged situation and will continue to worry and wonder about solutions to their child's reading problem when the answers are right here.

Therefore, we want you to take a moment to select one idea you like and commit to putting it into practice today. Referring back frequently to this power-packed little guide and experimenting with our tips and suggestions can become a worthwhile and enjoyable pastime. As you build into your life more and more of the recommended techniques you will start to see your child respond to your new approach by reading more and/or with more enjoyment. This will encourage you to continue to add to your toolbox until your process of helping your child to read more becomes the most natural thing in the world.

To fully ignite your own motivation, be sure not to skip over the previous chapter where we presented a research analysis of children's literacy by the National Education Association. That information may help you reach the place where putting our suggestions into practice becomes easy and natural.

Reading is a portal to personal growth like no other. It opens you up to previously unknown aspects of reality, expands your imagination, enhances your knowledge of life – of people, places, and things – and can be a source of endless joy, interest and entertainment through-out your lifetime. Give your child the gift of loving to read and they will forever thank you for it.

-

Did You Enjoy This Book?

Dear Reader,

I hope you enjoyed *The Reading Advantage: Quick & Easy Ways to Transform Your Child into a Passionate Reader!* I wrote this small book because I feel strongly about the importance of reading in childhood. Not only is reading a fulfilling pastime that can continue to bring joy throughout life, but it is also correlated with greater education, success and well-being in adulthood.

If you would like to recommend *The Reading Advantage* to other parents on Amazon, please take a moment to write a brief review. Thank you in advance! I appreciate it very much.

Wishing you the very best!

Strawberry Shakespeare

About the Author

Strawberry Shakespeare was born and educated in New York City where she received a master's degree and doctoral training in clinical psychology. While working in the mental health field, she returned to her original love – writing – and is now a bestselling children's author and screenwriter.

Saving Bluestone Belle, Shakespeare's debut novel, is a delightful comic-adventure for ages 8-12 and has been a book club selection, a featured attraction and an award winner at children's book groups, book fairs, book festivals and animal rights conferences across the country. Her other bestselling children's fiction include the enchanting short story collection, *The Cloud Horse & Other Stories,* and her newest release, the unforgettable tale *Hope's Horse: The Mystery of Shadow Ridge.*

Shakespeare was interviewed by reporters at the Animal Rights National Conference in Los

Angeles. What follows is a quote from that interview.

"How we treat the least among us is an indication of who we really are as a culture. Too often, horses are viewed as a disposable commodity rather than as faithful companions and helpmates of man. I was horrified by reports of their rampant abuse and exploitation by the horse slaughter industry, and decided to highlight this issue in my children's books. My hope is that these stories will inspire young people to take a stand against cruelty toward horses and other animals."

Read on to discover the children's books by Strawberry Shakespeare that your child is sure to love.

Children's Books by Strawberry Shakespeare

SAVING BLUESTONE BELLE
(Second Edition)

Saving Bluestone Belle is a contemporary, horse-themed novel for young readers by bestselling author Strawberry Shakespeare. This teacher-approved, award-winning comic-adventure is guaranteed to *make your child laugh out loud and keep turning the pages with breathless excitement.*

Saving Bluestone Belle tells about a stolen white horse and the ten-year-old boy who hits the road to rescue her. Along the way, young Homer goes up against an evil rancher and his wacky henchmen, only to be held captive in an underground fortress where he must use his quirky ingenuity to escape before it is too late!

This Disney-style story has been a featured attraction at children's book clubs, book fairs, book festivals and animal rights conferences across the country. It teaches children to be true to themselves and to care for the vulnerable creatures among us. Both avid and reluctant readers, boys and girls alike, will love the emphasis on snappy dialogue and fast-moving, action-oriented narrative.

The second edition of this popular book has been updated and enhanced by a new cover and two additional interior illustrations, bringing the total number of original works by talented contemporary artist Mike Bilz, to 12. With its rollicking tale and delightful art, *Saving Bluestone Belle* is certain to thoroughly entertain the horse kids among you as well as the entire family.

Saving Bluestone Belle is a 154 page novel for ages 8-12. The new second edition is available on Amazon in two formats: Kindle and paperback. The first edition hardcover collectible is also available on Amazon.

HOPE'S HORSE
The Mystery of Shadow Ridge

In this exciting new release by Strawberry Shakespeare, a 12-year-old girl, accompanied by the wild mustang she calls a friend, is drawn into a decades-old mystery surrounding the scary 'man on the mountain' and a strange metallic object buried in the mountain wilderness.

HOPE'S HORSE: The Mystery of Shadow Ridge, by bestselling children's author Strawberry

Shakespeare, is a captivating, horse-themed adventure novel for young readers ages 9-12. Set in the California Eastern Sierras, it tells the story of twelve-year-old Hope Miller and her wild mustang, Tango.

While recovering from the death of her beloved grandfather, who shared her love of horses, Hope is forbidden by her parents to go on the mountain alone or be anywhere near the wild horses she adores. So the girl keeps her horse, Tango, a secret from her parents, and rides him on the mountain without their knowledge.

On one of these outings, she and Tango evade evil poachers only to face a scary old mountain man. Escaping in a mad dash up the dark side of the mountain, they discover a mysterious metal object buried on Shadow Ridge. Hope instinctively knows her find is important and that she should tell her parents about it. But if she tells, she would also have to reveal the truth about her and Tango, and would probably never see him again.

A surprising turn of events merges the destinies of Hope, Tango and the old man on the mountain during a life-threatening confrontation with dangerous horse poachers. The resulting explosion of action, excitement, heartbreak and, ultimately, joyous healing is a must-read experience for the whole family and for every kid who loves adventure and horse stories.

HOPE'S HORSE: The Mystery of Shadow Ridge is a novel for readers ages 9-12 by Strawberry Shakespeare. It is currently available on Amazon in Kindle and print editions.

THE CLOUD HORSE
& Other Stories

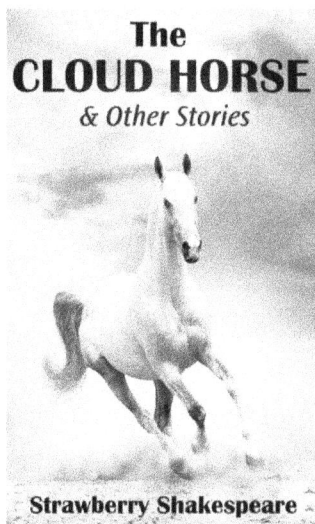

The
CLOUD HORSE
& Other Stories

Strawberry Shakespeare

Your horse-loving kids ages 8-12 will also absolutely love **The Cloud Horse & Other Stories** *by Strawberry Shakespeare and C. J. Dennis. This delightful volume contains three unforgettable and uplifting stories for children.*

Boys and girls of all ages who can't get enough of horses and adventure will adore the title story,

"The Cloud Horse," an exhilarating yarn about a kid who is whisked away on the back of a flying horse!

Based on "The Boy Who Rode into the Sunset," by Australian author C. J. Dennis, this classic tale is a personal favorite of children's author Strawberry Shakespeare.

In her quest to bring it to modern audiences, Shakespeare made several valuable enhancements to the original. These include creating an evocative new story title, designing a beautiful book cover, rightfully transforming the story into a novelette by dividing it into eight colorfully-named chapters and penning a fascinating chapter on the life and times of C. J. Dennis, all of which render this magical fable more meaningful and enjoyable than ever.

This volume also contains "White Fire" and "The Appaloosa Colt," two extraordinary short stories by bestselling children's author Strawberry Shakespeare. Readers of all ages will be enchanted by these mystical and inspiring tales.

The Kindle and paperback editions of *The Cloud Horse & Other Stories* are available on Amazon.com.

All of the children's horse books by Strawberry Shakespeare make perfect gifts for young readers. Order them now. Kids treasure these bestselling tales and so will you!

Free Gift

THE APPALOOSA COLT
by
Strawberry Shakespeare

When young Katie begins a volunteer job at the local horse rescue, her life changes in an amazing way. You'll take the journey with Katie as she goes from the painful low of an unjust accusation to the high of an impossible dream coming true; all of this while she is also awakening to her extraordinary ability with horses – a gift she never knew she had!

As our thanks to all the caring parents who have read *The Reading Advantage: Quick & Easy Ways to Transform Your Child into a Passionate Reader!,* we would like you to have the bonus short fiction ebook, "The Appaloosa Colt." This charming selection from Strawberry Shakespeare's bestselling short story collection for ages 8-12, *The Cloud Horse & Other Stories,* is certain to delight horse kids of all ages. Go to http://bit.ly/theappaloosacolt to download your free ebook now.

www.ingramcontent.com/pod-product-compliance
Lightning Source LLC
Chambersburg PA
CBHW060036050426
42448CB00012B/3029